Favorite Poems
55 New Poems

Favorite Poems

55 New Poems

An Eagle Falcon Publication

By

Dalward J DeBruzzi

E-BookTime, LLC
Montgomery, Alabama

Favorite Poems
55 New Poems

Library of Congress Control Number: 2018951170

ISBN: 978-1-60862-734-9

First Edition
Published October 2018
E-BookTime, LLC
6598 Pumpkin Road
Montgomery, AL 36108
www.e-booktime.com

A Little Mommie

I'm a little Mommie with much to do
My dollies need dressing and combing like
me and you
Then I feed them goodies and supper too

When they've eaten sometimes they're blue
To cheer them up I sing them lullabies and
rhymes
This lifts their moods prepares them for
bedtimes

They kneel down with devotion to say their
prayers
When finished Mommie puts them to bed
with care

by Dalwood J DeBruzzi

A Peddler

He comes around every year in his large
wagon full of wares to sell at retail
Pots, pans, thread, needles too numerous to
detail

His schedule is casual and not formal in any
way
May not appear same time on any day

Never gets bored or tired just up and goes
when inspired
Finds eager buyers where ever he visits
brings them goods they all desired

The carefree life of a peddler is exciting,
profitable gay
Sees the vast country while the customers
pay

Nothing good lasts as the peddler can
attest
As towns sprung up his appearance was
needed less and less

He is now extinct the commercial trade of endeavor
Only a remembrance of an era gone by forever

by Dalward J DeBruzzi

A Symphony

Petite tiny curvaceous girl with smile so
nice
With well formed man alongside ready to
take the ice

Poised ready the soft music triggers pair
into gliding motion
In perfect harmony they glide down the
arena smoothly running
Like one person so exact the illusion of a
shadow is cunning

They travel apart but in perfect unison of
movement
Every move exact precise little room for
improvement

Each move practiced as one delicate
mastered art
Their coordinated sweeps, turns, lifts,
gravity playing a part

A display of skill and beauty raising her
twirling in the air
Then gently lowering her safely with
dashing dare

Speeding rushing twirling as one a perfect
tandem
Then solo spinning then together nothing
random

Dinking dipping swirling slashing in ballet
style
With athletic art form each maneuver a
tense trial

A twin burst of speed each flight 3 turns
gravity in compliance
Alighting smoothly with seeming psychic
guidance

Between his legs over his head across his
chest again over his head skidding to
a stop
To thunderous applause taking deserved
accolades and earned praise what a
thrill clawing for the top

Maybe even a medal this time competing in winter Olympics the pinnacle for the pair
Aspiring for the gold "do we dare?"

by Dalward J DeBruzzi

Asunder

Life over no incentive to continue, rumors
started grew
Love dissolved lived in denial then love flew

Admonished and accused maidenly mate
No mild condemnation will do for asunder of
marriage fate

Declared she made me a cuckold of ridicule
And tho marriage is lost, my honor dignity too
Those losses I grieve though not losing you

Having partial attention from one you hold
dear is
Purgatory on earth with great despair
Tragic and miserable with agony no worth
or fanfare

It's better to empty the abode of unfaithful
incivility
Reform one's life dismiss vulnerability and
humility

Readjusted my life licked my wounds
surgical removal of toxic memories
Erasing nightmares cleansed mind no
apologies

Discovered time heals though wounds deep
and painful
Each morrow sun brighter hopes and
attitude gainful

Time as the catalyst I finally am whole in
body and mind
Discovered no matter the hurt myself I will
find

by Dalward J DeBruzzi

Awkward

I was diligently hoeing in a long corn row
Stupidly I goofed stepped on a hoe

With anger it swooped up broke my nose
It had a right I erred I suppose

Though it was my fault and the hoe wasn't
to blame
I spewed profanity with a vicious tirade to
my shame

Although I over reacted like an immature
fool
Could anyone suspect a farm implement
could turn into a dangerous tool

by Dalward J DeBruzzi

Bees

There are drones who do little around a hive
And yet the queen bee and workers thrive

Queen fertilized perpetuates population of
hive
After mating every drone mated with queen
will not survive

Queen is the largest, then drone, then worker
Between drone and worker drone is a shirker

In 30 minutes queen mates with 20 drones
produces
Thousands of eggs all drones will perish
after queen seduces

Workers pollinate collect the nectar from
each flower
Many workers lost each day weary, tired
broken wings no power

Workers mix nectar with enzyme in mouth
makes honey
Stored as wax worth money

Six months of short life bee makes 1/12 of a
teaspoon of honey
Honey produced by colony main mission of
bee keeper makes life sunny

What would we do without drones, workers
and queens
Do without honey, no flowers and drabness
it seems

by Dalward J DeBruzzi

Betrayal

To you my love I consecrate
The loftiest esteem I can generate

Your loyalty trust confidence love you
placed in me
Was unreturned dashed to the ground like
wasted scree

Scrambled to marry when threatened with
desertion
For molesting young girl thought an amusing
diversion

When first wed loved each other dearly
treated you selfishly with unkind
unilateral unfair behavior
Consideration for your wifely needs ignored
only my own gratification how
inhumane no savior

Dictatorial demanding with little respect
and love
No blessings no consideration help from
above

Ashamed to recall my bad attitude so insensitive and mean
My motives unclear but surely unclean and seen

Your parents believed in me entrusted you to me
I was treacherous to all unplanned or not it didn't have to be

Deluded myself the fault was yours for years
Thinking back how I caused you grieving tears

Lying to myself gave false innocence and undeserved peace
Now suffering from acknowledged sins of my wanton fleece

by Dalward J DeBruzzi

Bomb Shelter

Dull thuds and muffled explosions heard in
bomb shelter today
To and fro up and down in darkness pacing
midst of fray

Deprived of childhood and also a sitter
When cheated naturally left feeling
despairing and bitter

Was fed in hospital from a stainless steel tray
With luck and good fortune only a short stay

In wonder of man's intellect can he discover
the means
To exercise magic and discover needed
palliating extremes

If one could find the catalystic principle to
appeal to illusive enduring peace
Could dismiss shelters emergency hospital
visits disrupted lives misery could cease

by Dalward J DeBruzzi

Boopsie's Pet

Little Boopsie's dog was small lively and
hairy
Creamy white round as a ball and merry

Little Boopsie's dog eats very little we agree
The reason a fat dog she doesn't want to be

She only loves bones hunts them all day
Gnawing a bone keeps her weight away

Boopsie's pet loves her never gives her
sweat
She wags her tail with love, never a threat

Boopsie's dog runs gets sticks and balls
Comes running obediently when Boopsie
calls

by Dalward J DeBruzzi

Charley Crab

My name is Charley Crab
My life is anything but drab

Each day is excitement unfurled
My colony is one of four thousands species
in the world

We are adaptable we live in oceans lakes
fresh water streams and on land
In each environment we find life and living
just grand

It looks like I have 10 legs but I only have
eight
The front two are claws but can be used to
walk straight

I'm a medium sized crab live in Chesapeake
Bay
In a small colony by night and by day

Growing up to adulthood my growth gets stunted
Have to shed my hard cover to prevent being runted

This happens as often as my growth extends
When I'm at full growth shedding suspends

I may look slow but can move fast when need to
As my past dinners of snails, mussels, worms, clams and small crabs can assure you

Life of a crab is neither wholly dreary or cherry
If lucky we can live 28 years but of this longevity leery

We must avoid vultures, bald eagles, drum fish, striped bass all deadly in pursuit of dinner of me
Man, larger crabs and the blue crabs all eye me with glee

With all forms of life in the world the same
rule prevails
Life is longer for some, shorter for others,
shorter and fails

by Dalward J DeBruzzi

Costly Mistress

Mistress added costly in many ways indeed
My coyness overcome with craving need

My dread is real that creditors
Morph into forceful predators

Each tryst I'm charged is ill afforded at best
A fealty at your beholding feet in my zest

You demand the choicest food wines and suite
Homage is obedience from me you treat

With blended guilt dissatisfaction cheating on marriage vows that were taken
Marital purity dim and vague now shaken

Feeling remorseful and elated for combined reaction
Though detesting my predicament want my satisfaction

When periodic requests for more money made
Another economical adjustment bag lunch at desk now I'm afraid

As shipwrecks useless and undesirable
So my costly mistress lost allure and withered desire

Wished now for status quo to be
Home, wife, children, house no longer belongs to me

Couldn't afford costly mistress while I cavorted
Like useless shipwreck my fling is over and aborted

Living at the Y.M.C.A. is Spartan living and appalling
Recalling my poor judgment is penitent and galling

by Dalward J DeBruppi

Cynical Thieving Fox

A long tailed fox stole into the vineyard of
grapes
Stealing his food was his enhancement to
sates

He looked up at juicy tantalizing bunches to
eat
From his jaws dripped saliva expecting a
treat

He leaped up missed came down naught
Tried again and again still fruitlessly sought

Soon exhaustion no tidbits gained this day
Long yearning look up at unattainable prey

Curled his tail between his legs crawled away
Mumbled with cynicism "they probably were
sour grapes anyway"

by Dalward J DeBruzzi

Empathy

No matter profound grievous anguished
deep sorrow
Misery and pain cannot last indefinitely
sometimes fades on the morrow

Resolve it to pass will expend itself in time
Its rage will subside as receding gale or
fierce tempest will decline just fine

With time and determination you forget
things done
Eventually with concentration your troubles
you shun

I will act like a builder who works with
extreme care
Calculating my life with rule saw and square

If you're unselfish compassionate and for
others you live
Your destiny insured for others you did give

Troubles and woe lifelong companions on journey of life
Secret is suppress it burst through free of strife

by Dalward J DeBruzzi

Everyone

Secrets hidden locked away lapsed faded
memory
Buried in vault of forgetfulness some almost
a century

Tales revealed would sadden embarrass
maybe worse
Evil dark secrets serious not forgotten
known a curse

Shame is suppressed, acknowledged but
denied
Tainted deeds expunged memory decried

Presidents, clergy, doctors, lawyers too no
area excluded
With guarded sins stumble and fall included

Mistakes were made some consensual
some intrusive
All are enrolled in infamous contrition
results abusive

Eventful exposure visible on display
Total destruction grief and dismay

It's best cut your losses let your sordid
secrets drown die away
Resolve with contrition to change direction
rebirth a new day

by Dalward J DeBruzzi

Exotic Travels

Up into the tallest tree
Who climbed here but little me

Waved at the vast world with both hands
In all the corners of all the lands

Saw snow, glaciers, dunes of sand
Animals, clawed, horned, taloned on water and on land

The people, yellow, white, black, and red all colors with one quest in mind
Seek, find, feed, beings of their own kind

by Dalvard J DeBruzzi

Fairy Tales

In green dense thick forests where we
cannot see
The teeny fairies cavort romp in total glee

Most amusing little beings cute as they can
be
They dance, whirl twist leap in rapt reverie

They sing and tweet melodious tunes and
rhymes
Ever happy pleasant ebullient with good
times

Their chatter is different but engaging to
hear
Longer you listen the more to your heart
they endear

A little fellow special by name of Tintoc I
did meet
We became fast friends and exchanged
oaths discreet

I wish I could take Tintoc home a very
special fairy indeed
Put him on a memento shelf and announce
he's freed

"Freed he said", that's false conclusion
I know am that now with no confusion

After that day never found a fairy again was
memory in blunder
Was previous encounter fantasy or wonder

In the dense thick green forest I walk with
expectation
But fail to detect nary a fairy ever again by
detection

Is it memory failure that affects my wits on
end
Or did it never happen is forgetfulness the
trend

by Dalward J DeBruzzi

Famine

It's not a day dream I think but a cause to
think
Daily in areas children with ribs on display
are on starvation's brink

Some tots have wishes for a Christmas toy
While others cry for gnawing hunger pangs
to go away

Some children warble grace in thanks for
nutritious treasures of food
Ample in quantity not ubiquitous on the
planet not good

Others not thinking of bicycles, sleds or
toys just bread and meat
Tragedy is the absurdity of cause, children
most effected

Bountiful nourishment is scarce for some
global innocents we know neglected

Many tykes know daily hunger
Innocent tots hungry a bed at night in
proximity to where we live

Where we in reality near
Solution unfound tragedy a constant fear

by Dalward J DeBruzzi

Five Days to Paradise

Five days to paradise how I'll survive I don't know
So much to do overpowering new experience a real show

We ordered dinners gifts for wedding party condiments for connubial feast
Wanted everything perfect for friends and family for them they deserved none the least

Got home late nervous on edge
Got some rest renewed my pledge

Next day checked on reception hall decorated in decorous refinement and taste
It was colorful ornate beautiful and chaste

Arranged for a band to orchestrate at reception
Then a rental tuxedo good fit satisfaction

Final morning of our big day arrived not coy
It went amazingly smooth happiness and joy

Mr. and Mrs. what a glorious sound our
sumptuous wedding was heavenly crowned
We looked at each other with two feet on
the ground

It was a fabulous wedding more expensive
than we calculated
Now find a way to pay it off as soon as cost
evaluated

Love can be blind and cause resistance
It was worth the debt will pay it with
consistence

Love and happiness can't be purchased
You could fool me

Were both unemployed have no job in sight
Deep in debt can't pay rent buy food now
afright

She went home to mother to escape the mess
I fled to the bottle for relief from the stress

Our only bright peep hole in all this
Was the five days of happiness and perfect bliss

by Dalward J DeBruzzi

Forest Fire

Fire burning blazing in the dark night
Glowing crackling burning trees sending up
    billows of smoke a fright

Animals fleeing before relentless raging
    advancing front of fire
Countless men battling to hold all consuming
    destructive advance how they tire

Evacuation ordered palatial homes doomed
    to destruction
Fire widespread burning thousands of acres
    devastating property reduction

People crowding shelters no home no
    possessions
Sleeping on cots with deep moody
    depressions

Fire rages on many square miles now
    charred
Homes lost all possessions gone life as we
    knew it is marred

Fire finally under control and put out
Displaced devastated people stand and
shout

Survived the tragic ordeal to carry on
though grievous harm
Loss stronger faith embraced hath calmed
alarm

by Dalward J DeBruzzi

Handsome Mallard Duck

The sleek plump colorful Mallard duck
glossy green head
Was handsome and seemed to know it felt
pure bred

Waddled out of the water to and fro side to
side
On yellow skinned taut webbed feet with pride

Makes clicks wet sounds low and soft
From his round pointed yellow beak

Flinging last beads of water from his slick
sloping back
Looked regal handsome decided take him
home intact

Had to make a decision make him a pet
decided to put him in the oven
Instead baked him to perfection of his taste
we were a loven

by Dalward J DeBruzzi

Idealistic

I was young sweet natured pretty and
eighteen and felt I was called
Inspired with intense emotion to serve with
feelings enthralled

Investigated orders of nuns found poverty
service required
Felt the summons from God humility
celibacy desired

To be summoned is a gift an anointment
from above
Easily accomplished lived to serve with
complete love

As a novice did cooking cleaning studying
and praying
Year later convinced my life will be here am
staying

Felt tremors urges from bodily changes
Questioned my stance on celibacy ranges

Told mother superior my anguish need for
direction
She advised rededication more prayer
introspection

I prayed meditated fought with tenacity
Body rebelled demanded veracity

My natural urges were overwhelming
scourges
Threats to my novitiate no pacifying merges

No longer a novice in service of God couldn't
handle the celibacy demand of
abstention
Still devoutly religious family woman with
intention

by Dalward J DeBruzzi

Maturation

If sins you've committed are beyond pardoning
Time for circumspection alas a heart's
hardening

Need for contrition emphatic decision
Accounting for vacillating path repent acts
of remission

Repentance is painless if heart steadied
and trued
Correct direction on course with resolve
construed

Remorse now dismissed past behind with
gloom
Peace tranquility looked forward like
flowers in bloom

No longer will misstep or err new ethics
guiding fate
With soothing strokes rehabilitation will
nigh be late

by Dalward J DeBruzzi

Mistaken Identity

In early morn horizon lights up and dawn
does appear
A musical wren sings sweetly, melodiously
with cheer

To regular early morn passersby he is daily
performing
Flits and hops dives while warbling sweetly
dispelling mourning

Without fail he performs each break of day
like sworn call to a mission
Neither hot nor cold daunts his commission

Small feathered singing bird appearance
thought to be same one each new
sunrise entering play
Surprise it was different one each day

A community of wrens alternated doing the
task daily
To the delight but unwary audience who had
only praises to say gaily

by Dalward J DeBruzzi

My Desire

Strolling along easy life in journey with light
step
Was aimless reckless lack of directed pep

Then one sober day serious assessment in a
lonely place
Sorted out partially with fractional facts
face to face

Mate for body to motivate my desire to
blossom
New interest in life with wife in mind no
need to play possum

Behold finally found her knew her blushed
to admit
Was foolish to have waited so long to submit

Faltering mind wandering gyrating in daze
Brightened in warmth at contentment in
amaze

For others still lost as I once was without direction
Hopefully don't wait as I did and promptly make selection

by Dalward J DeBruzzi

My Prayers

You're kindly generous we thank you for the
waking light
For the restful peaceful slumber through the
long night

Gratitude for food, your guidance and
watchful care
All the things that free us from a life of despair

Thank you for showing us how to be good
Clearing the path enabling us to be pious as
we should

Each day we try harder to do as you say
If we tend to waver with your guidance and
resolve we pray

Our goal and salvation is eternally blessed
sanctification
Hopefully perpetual life with the blessing of
purification

by Dalward J DeBruzzi

My Princess

In thy heart there is no guile
Only purity of your smile

Thy skin be fair
Ornamented with silken corn colored hair

Untold beauty graces thy gentle form
fashioned with careful selection
From artists easel or sculptors chiseled
symmetry in human perfection

Your cheeks of creamy complexion their
beauty transcendent
When I first felt love for you its power was
overwhelming drugging resplendent
I became dependent

Dignity honor worth enveloped with pure
love is enduring
My benediction dismisses restriction revering
my princess sates my adoration in psychical
realms insuring

by Dalward J DeBruzzi

My Rescue

It's been many long hard years
Copious amounts salty bitter tears

When I plodded along the tainted trail of sin
Cringed in shame and chagrin

Shudder humiliated fully understand
Foul sinner I've been deserver of reprimand

With self introspection gazed into mirror
Saw someone I disliked no endearer

With sharpened objective perspective
Acquired altered ethics oft ignored and deplored

Felt surging acceptance of new destiny and direction
Feel acceptable cleaner more self affection

People now greet me warmly to my face
Former behavior in life not a trace

Pleased with new found contentment in present mode
Fetters of weakness did effectively erode

by Dalward J DeBruzzi

My Resurrection

Life felt over didn't care to live, when rumors
grew
Lived in denial then faced the reality then I
knew

Was seething irate grievous and hurt had no
gentle condemnation for asunder of
marriage fate
You exposed me a cuckold of ridicule scorn
shame lost honor betrayed by my mate

Partial attention from one you hold dear is
not matrimony
Fosters resentment, pejorative feelings
acrimony

It's better to empty the abode of proven
treachery and incivility
Avoid vulnerabilities and possible future
humility

When the outlook is darkest revival is borne
Like a medical procedure we experience
removal of thorn

Life will cure with time as catalyst to heal
Finally able to feel able can face future now
with zeal

Time purges the poisonous memories of yore
Though the wounds be deep painful grievous
and sore

by Dalward J DeBruzzi

My Retreat

Rural rustic little traveled lane is my
wonderful find
Peaceful relaxing my favorite cherished
kind

Minimal noise clack and clatter devoid of
frantic race
Strolling peacefully languidly to each
secluded place

Copse of stately trees, bees, birds and
flowers
Provides protective cover like being in lofty
towers

Serenity golden in this country side of
heaven mystically sent
To permit the luxury of taking a path with
no intent

Languorous visit over my thoughts will have
recalled
Each nook and niche I contentedly visited
enthralled

Residual pleasantries of remembrances shall remain
In recurring daydreams of the past inspiring refrain

When again drawn to stroll the hallowed path of little traveled lane no choices
I drift into tranquil peace with absence of din and voices

by Dalward J DeBruzzi

Ode to Ma and Dad

Dad's father died of gangrene when he was
eight
His mother remarried with step father poor
fate

Life of drudgery work no abate in toil
Learning to third grade ran away at thirteen
to foil

Married Laura few years later with tender
romance
Two struggling youngsters no support help
askance

No guidance, no start, few clothes is all
Love and support of each other sustained
them no ball

Neither educated facing living, surviving by
wits
Competing in brutal, unyielding greedy
world one admits

Hard workers scratched out survival with
tenacity
Became salesman selling soap such audacity

No education, no work experience
With native intellect made a living as
salesman, what courage!

Now railroad man, but depression hit lost
job, helpless no welfare, food stamps
charities
Then house, despair, three children what to
do?

Brave youngsters undaunted by problems
and averses
Packed a trailer hit the road not stymied by
reverses

Left Ashland for Milwaukee where jobs
might be found
Not knowing if at night they would sleep on
the ground

Found apartment late next day worked hard
to contend
Deroached the next few days had little
money to spend

John went looking for work for days kept
trying
Persisted kept applying

Embarrassed asking for help in filling out
papers
After initial humiliation humbling tapers

Found employment at Heil Co. as welder,
Was great worker dedicated to his family

Two years later called back to railroad in
Chicago
Rented home mother with enterprise rented
rooms

John and Laura were uneducated true but
irrelevant
Their natural instincts were lofty and pure

Educated four children through high school
a coup
Children fortunate to have had them for true

These two beautiful resourceful souls were
inspirations
They conquered all with natural fine
motivations

Every sacrifice they made was an
expression of love
Not in words but in essence from above

by Dalward J DeBruzzi

Perseverance

When reverses are pressing you're taking it
on the chin
Recharge if you must but don't relent and
give in

Most know sometimes from this learns
Life is challenging complex with angles
twists and turns

Many troubles and failures can be turned
around
By thinking working and standing your ground

Stick to a solution courage you must show
You may be victorious with one more firm
blow

You're never aware how close to victory you
sit
The indelible message to remember you
never quit

by Dalward J DeBruzzi

Preference

I like to watch people in entertainment who
look like me
Whether your Asian, white or black matters
not, you agree

It's called preference an individual right
Not to be confused with squabble of racial
fight

Each person has right to exert their choices
Despite any objections to apply their voices

by Dalwand J DeBruppi

Restoratives

After bleak trying frustrating dispiriting day
How restorative to hear healing words I love
you to soften the fray

When things tend to darken unravel begin to
fall apart
Your words and support bolster my faltering
heart

When burdens increase become unbearable
to endure
Your stalwart shoulder I seek dispelling
censure

When things become vague iffy in question
The words I love you aid in palliative digestion

Precious sensitive restorative words
ameliorates depressants
Their effect without words means that
someone does care.

by Dalvard J DeBruppi

River of No Return

Parting can be painful from a loved one for
many a mournful reasons
Angst and melancholy supersede the
seasons

Destined to meet no more we grievously
lament
Despondency despair for our deep emotion
profound and fervent

Wringing hearts, wringing hands of surging
regret desire mislaid
Things now forsook relegated to memories
that fade

Are thee no more My friend? My soul mate?
My Love?
A blurred vacuum encompasses my fragile
life no longer binded from above

We've parted the tears now steady will
remain
Brightness golden memories eternal
treasures will sustain

by Dalward J DeBruzzi

Secrets

Secrets buried in closets are common in
kind
They are concealed in bad memories locks
on your mind

Some are small and some are large but all
etched in time
With forgetfulness rationalization can
dismiss the infraction or crime

Details revealed would sadden embarrass
maybe worse
Dark secrets serious not forgotten a
memory curse

Shame is suppressed guilt acknowledged
then denied
Erasing deeds from recall defied

Secrets encrypted in closed minds are not
rare as you think at all
If some would be exposed many would fall

Presidents, clergy, leading community
leaders no category excluded
All with some guarded secrets known only
to their recall definitely included

Mistakes in judgment willing or
unintentional matters not
All accounts outstanding no plot

Sudden exposure in visible display
Causes grief total destruction and total
dismay

Most cut their losses bury tainted deeds
deep and far away
Resolve to carry forth shoulder the burden
look to a new day

by Dalward J DeBruzzi

Snow Flakes!

Snow flakes, tiny fluffy, drifting down in
agile grace
Sailing, floating, fluttering, in leisurely pace
In swirls they travel, high, low, on around
How I wish I could grasp you
Before you hit the ground
On second thought?
Later no sun to moderate giving flakes
longer duration
Cold floods in allowing snow deepen in
accumulation
Hours beyond roads glutted and clogged
impassable beyond repair
First light white dusting then gradual depth
of despair
Swirling relentless ogre bent on a
surreptitious snare
All this dismay because the gentle fragile
little snow flakes grow angry and vicious in
a way not fair

Little snow flakes with a pardon for longer life
Can become a monster of disruption and deadly as an assassin with a knife

by Dalward J DeBruppi

Solitude

Give me a path distant from dense masses
Away from the din cacophony carbon dioxide
    gases

Give me license to travel to roam far
    explore sedate paths
In leisurely quietude less minor wraths

Where measurement is calculated in dells
    and valleys
Copses vast and mountains where solitude
    in man dallies

When pleasure registered in mind for ever
Peace contentment serenity effortless
    endeavor

Broad stretches of expansive area sought
To continue to regale in pensive recall and
    thought

by Dalvard J DeBruzzi

Steering Through Life

Confusion, mind adrift coping with intrusiveness
The oarsman slackens hold on wheel with unwariness

Course is altered unsure and faulted
Remembrance of a complete thought long gone
Craft into waters strange entering new dawn

Breezes wafted in sunshine gleamed in freckle spray
Course unsure unconfirmed only trial and error then pray

Lives are chronicled in same imaginary semblance of order
Realize it's an element of hope luck fate to life's path fraught with disorder

At ripened old age old man loved crumbs of unsure existence
Was far greater than he thought despite no resistance

**Like a ship without perfect navigation, old
mariner stumbled toward the obituary
In penitential loneliness goes erring or true
to church cemetery**

by Dalward J DeBruzzi

Stricken Maiden

In a distant locality far away and in another
 time
A deep concealed pool whose depth was in
 rhyme

Reverberated melodious tunes to soothe a
 maiden's heart
The clear pool enveloped submerged cardiac
 fibrillations from the start

She surged with intense passion intending
 to ravish, is it best to dive, or to climb
 and soar
In matters of the heart it's indecisive maybe
 yes or abhor

The way to go will be felt in vibes
When emotions begin to pour with profound
 gush and facility

Rarified air is indistinct and unsteady
stricken maiden groping for lucidity
Seeks to refresh as a lonely flower
untouched by her hapless unfortunate lack of floridity

The sagging spirits of a depressed mind in absence
Yearns we who import loving shares salience

by Dalward J DeBruzzi

The Country Boy

Leaving the farm to seek my fortune and
        future
Must overcome emotional bleeding with
        strong suture

Farewell to farm home mom dad sister too
Kissing embracing with affectionate saying
        "I love you"

Panorama parades in front of me so clear
Ist day of school... Ist tricycle... Ist love in
        third grade
Parental advice keep resolve work hard
        don't let ambition fade

With honest toil keep faith be loyal and true
From parents were gems and treasures
        worthy to pursue

No lack of familiar credos grew up living
        them daily
Were worthy noble practiced them gaily

Felt moral character adequate to function
unscathed in city steeped in frailties
Big city exciting wild confusion avoided
intemperate drinking, drugs and girls
who ignored deities

Led clean life, church every Sunday in my
pew
From farm to city both had good points and
close in choice
No fresh beef pork lamb or veggies off the
vine in this city no voice

Stern lesson learned in my exodus to the city
Some things you will like and some offer no
pity

Calculate the gain and the loss and proceed
to a decision
If tally book lop sided demands a revision

Lesson learned from my jaunt to city
Imperative to gauge what is gained and lost
If tally book lopsided equity tossed

Revision of plans required to restore to
placid existence
I'm back on the farm with all had before
plus wife in addition

by Dalward J DeBruzzi

The Dance Hall

She was popular in great demand
Her dance card excessively manned

Cowardly stealthy seclusion behind a palm tree peeking
Heart pinning head spinning with want unable to speak up
Inability to state my case each time you passed lived on the crumbs of your vision my empty cup

Sweet visions vicarious thoughts of success
Sober fact pleasures nonexistent success a blur

Courage collected felt adequate one night advanced
To tender my case so entranced

Natural voice fled replaced by a trill
"May I have this dance miss?" I wanted my fill

Without looking at me she said "I'm booked up tight"
Having seen her up close my perspective got right

She was older that I thought with caked makeup hiding faults just fine
Released from my yen now no longer did pine

Never cower afraid to find the facts instead of tacit reaction
She was kinda pretty though kindly sweet as spice
Was a smooth talented dancer and very nice

Learned that always speak up to state a case
Don't waste futile effort doing nothing won't get on base

Admit she was rather pretty personality sugar and spice
A great dancer warm and friendly and really nice

by Dalward J DeBruzzi

The Farm Maiden

The fair maiden on the 1st of May snuggled
with her beau in the soft frizzly hay
Laughed lived now back to the fray

Tend chores skipped into barn cows content
chewing
Took a bucket sat doing milking foaming
spurting into pail
Each filled pail poured into dairy milk can
for sale

One chore finished she skipped to the garden
Hoed between the corn rows for hours and
hours
Suppered then tended to an array of flowers

The fair milk maiden did all this with zeal
Life for her on the farm is real no tedium or
bores
Following morn started feeding chickens
then went through list of chores

The work schedule she likes soon to have
help
Beau to be husband and partner for life

Fair maiden though not married yet loved
the daily visit to hayloft spot
Every one lives a little before they live a lot

by Dalward J DeBruzzi

The Hero

I joined the army at eighteen years old
Trained hard learned how to be good soldier
bold

Land mine blasted my half track took off
both legs
Sent home promptly as recovery begs

My depression is deep hurtful and damaging
with persistence
Despite doctors of medicine and psychiatry
assuaging assistance

I found war is not what I thought
But my country called I responded and fought

I earned no significant medals of any kind
Am now a cripple a new life to find

There are thousands like me broken, maimed
seeking new means
To cope and renew dreams

In the rehabilitation facility I spend my efforts finding what I can do
It's a way to cope with life's challenge it's most I can construe

Everyone calls me a hero I dismiss the description
I just did my duty like everyone should without conscription

Thanks to all who help me through "Wounded Warriors"
You're generous and good helping me regain my existence your support is life saving

I need the help to surmount new barriers
Thank you thank you thank you

by Dalward J DeBruzzi

The Homesteaders

We lived in Altoona a small town in the East
Hungered for a place of our own acquisition
a feast

Bought a Conestoga wagon loaded it with
flour
Tea, salt, rice, coffee, corn and all our
possessions
Joined with other wagons made a train left
in an hour

We left in the spring to favor mild season
Traveling with favorable weather the reason

We traveled five to ten miles a day traveling
not easy when woman with child and
children to caress
We endured privations of great discomfort
and duress

We traveled hard crossed rivers and
mountains sometimes in harsh
weather
Endured illness scarce food stayed close to
camp as if on a tether

When night camp made children played
games to amuse
Told stories sang songs for boredom to
diffuse

A jolly community sprung up sharing
hardships and task
The common comforting thought in our own
land we bask

We toiled together for water wood fruits
berries and game
There was no shirking attached to that was
no shame

We arrived in heaven staked our plot whole
family pitched in to do their part
Planted plowed hoed readying first crop a
start

The first year hardest a bountiful yield
Prepare soil carefully get ready the field

Then orchards cows sheep pigs chickens
steers
My family now secure have no fears

Deed to the homestead I own it outright it's
mine
Our trek was worth it now everything's fine

by Dalward J DeBruzzi

The Loss

Despite streams of misfortune and
insurmountable woe
Stay resolved steady opportunity for your
faith to grow

There's hope for morrow if character
unyielding and firm
Faced adversity, reverses with spirit strong
no concern

When morality weakens the erosion begins
Though minor at first the infection needs
pathology
Reaches critical mass then approaches
apostasy

They have broken down your moral fences
Swept away your maidenly defenses

Though once chaste, pure, virtuous and pious
Now tried, used, soiled gaining only
disdainful ires

Despite descent from grace quickly say you love me
My heart still yearns and aches for need of thee

When you're in my sight my thirst for you does multiply
Despite all that's past my true love will meliorate and rectify

If feelings are a haven for a loved one provided
Fall from grace is temporary dismissed and abided

by Dalward J DeBruzzi

The Quest

Oh refined judgment don't be late
Quandary is what to love what to hate

It seems simple which choice to choose
But lack of or faulty judgment sometimes can confuse

Shall I do this or that or something radical
Dally waste time or try something piratical

It's difficult to pick the path that is correct
Knowing it may lead to failure as well as success

Life is somewhat of a gamble nothing for sure to depend on
Be aware of human natures frailties don't fall for a con

It's a long drawn out journey with no guarantees and insurance
A path with pit falls, obstacles, snares to deny preference

If the journey is mature and health wealth is present
You were fortuitous in your early selection
Not knowing the accuracy of your projection

by Dalward J DeBruzzi

The Singer

Warbling wren glides and swoops across
the starry sky
Gentle wafting breeze carries melodious
lilting song on high

Twisting diving turning while giving avian
melody with perfect notes repose
relax and lay
Wren swings and glides in swooping turns
awash with tides and no delay

Tweets so sweet harmonious delighting
throngs
Wrens nesting in early spring tweeting their
lilting musical chirping beautiful songs

By lucky chance may hear the entire
concert at its best
Hopefully will prolong

So lively pulsating pleasing unique artistic
offering therapeutic with encouraging
rest
Little considerate feathery friend toils to
give his best

Language heard is delightful tweets
Interpreted deciphered all fine treats

Sitting neath waving branches green and
content
Was graced with fine melodies pleasure
was intent

It must be experienced to feel what I do
Words not enough to explain it to you

by Dalward J DeBruzzi

The Witch

I have tried most earnestly to be other than
a witch
But change eluded me I could not switch

I had a fine spouse, two beautiful heirs in
wait
My failure to see worth in my world, most
profligate

To know one's shortcomings is painful
indeed
Powerless to correct, and to intercede

Prophesizes ill tidings with full recognition
Consequences must he expected as
retribution

Change came, not to me for alteration for
better
But for those in affinity in direct fetter

Old wrinkled, all alone, isolated from all
Lesson learned to late with reluctant pall

Inability or refusal to be adaptive and
affable
Is foolish, tragic, costly not laughable

by Dalward J DeBruzzi

Tiny Black Girl

In central Congo in Bukama was a twenty
thatched hut village near the river
A little black girl named Tambella lived
happily despite alligators, dangerous
animals never a shiver

She was Bantu of the Barudi tribe a happy
people peaceful, friendly, hospitable
They loved their crafts daily life led a life
imitable

Tambella was 3 feet tall with large sparkling
eyes
Tiny pug nose, glorious black fluffy hair with
ties

Was painted in white designs head adorned
with bandanna of yellow
Her well formed lips heart shaped face
sweet and mellow

Was a beauteous child with her black
glowing freshness for all to see
Belongs anywhere would be appreciated
with fanfare
A recognized misplacement that is tragic
and unfair

To appreciate her startling special
uniqueness
One would have to see her to appreciate the
alert keenness

Beauty is secluded everywhere but asserts
itself with
Passive presence by its own force and
essence

By any uniform standard of worldly measure
Little Tambella would be a treasure

by Dalward J DeBruzzi

Together

She strode proudly at my side devoted and
glowing in pride
A startled young girl newly crowned bride

Beginning was incredible all harmonious
loyal and love
Her dedication overwhelming as anointed
from above

Though sitting in silence content without
speech
Affecting thrilling the other to beseech

Together at night by hour by minute in our
ivory tower
Shut of the world no malignity our love will
never sour

Isolated we create peace and beauty
inviolate
Our marriage is pure solid in a realm of
luxuriate

Relationship endured now old grey decrepit
in mobility
Fresh current vibrant is still exciting no
futility

Thro our lifetime we've had our continuous
glory
A fitting climax to a wonderful life story

by Dalward J DeBruzzi

What Victory!

Armies appearance caused fixed staring
gazes
Fear rejection awed reaction conjuring
malaises

Up and down the streets all lights are out
yet brilliant light
From roaring fires cast blinding flashes
showing blight

All this while sounds of pounding stomping
feet
Engulf the citizens presence no longer
discreet

Ubiquitous tendrils curling twisting upward
from embers dying palls
While dusty particles fall on roads
sidewalks and fractured walls

Troops trod by homes and edifices blazing
infernos
Observing their destructive effectiveness or
so

Flames reignite anew with evil persistent
mission
Troops once prominent luster faded their
victory complete
City in heaps of rubble smoldering in
destruction no honorable feat

Women children men homeless little or
nothing to eat
Suffering widespread victors marched on to
repeat

Victory in territory gained loss in human
dignity for victor and vanquished both
deep in strife
Loss of humanity is self defeating leaving
stains for life

by Dalward J DeBruzzi

Which Way?

Life's torturous path evidenced by constant
moans
Disappointments broken oaths and fractured
bones

Dreams bodies broken spirits aimless deluge
of confusion
Nigh day to day existing with warped
delusion

Sitting in school desks year after year
running wild
Lying cheating stealing wandering delinquent
child

Older thought deep woke saw need for
redemption
Reenrolled in high school at 20 excelled
with goal of resurrection

Discovered beauty of knowledge achievable
goals within sight
Aspired profession exerted required effort
paid dues right

My fortuitous luck in never getting a record
was a blessing of grace
If happened would have derailed my pace

Graduated summa cum laude was
valedictorian too
Smug feeling made proper decisions when
needed new view

Following meandering track of life one need
after another emerges
Stable now right trail found gaping vacuum
in existence at new plateau
Additional urge surges in time does grow

Identified my lack addressed the craving
need
Down the curling path can say I did succeed

Profession wife four children lovely bright
All because stumbled on paths that were
right

by Dalward J DeBruzzi

Whimsical Rain

Some raindrops are tiny and hardly seen at all
While others are large with saturating pall

At times it's not a drop only a faint mist
Not droplets yet dampness and wetness will
persist

When it rains lightly and your slicker is
protecting you
Feels refreshingly pleasant until it's through

Sometimes it's slashing and whips your face
fiercely
Or maybe fall gently with soothing simplicity

It's sneaky at times surprises on sunny days
gone bad
Catches you unwary no umbrella to be had

It pleases the farmers and most others it
makes glad
The alternative is no rain how gloomily sad

by Dalward J DeBruzzi

Winter

Winter for me descends like a dark
enveloping cloud
A desultory gloomy inadequate shroud

Each day grows darker longer turning
moods surly
It's a quirk of the mind an object of
imagination purely

It's a futile gesture to combat the cold
season
I light my lights in rebellion tho I'm freezin

Tho disgruntled as I be not all share my
displeasure
Many love skiing, skating, sledding or
playing in snow for pleasure

Wives clean cook bear children season
discounted
Aspects of living can't avoid must be
accounted

Fact cannot be denied it's too evident once more
Like winter the best some passion unable to ignore

Warm weather devotees also we agree it's true
Concede each has his choice to satisfy his view

Despite this concession to independent selection
Stand fast in my objection to cold and darkness in rejection

by Dalvard J DeBruzzi

Would This Last?

My live in girlfriend says she loves me so
With all my heart this I know

My heart is in angst when she's not close by
Enduring her absence is hard but I try

She pleads wedding, now is the thing to do
I think to do that would be wonderful too

But a huge obstacle denies this connubial
bliss
We both have the drive and desire but age
amiss

We're unable to thwart bodily changes that
surely do come on
She is forty-three, I am eighty one

by Dalward J DeBruzzi

CPSIA information can be obtained
at www.ICGtesting.com
Printed in the USA
FFHW02n2330221018
48939971-53165FF